Note: All activities in this book should be performed with adult supervision. Common sense and care are essential to the conduct of any and all activities, whether described in this book or not. Neither the author nor the publisher assumes any responsibility for any injuries or damages arising from any activities.

KINGFISHER
An imprint of Kingfisher Publications Plc
New Penderel House, 283-288 High Holborn, London WC1V 7HZ
www.kingfisherpub.com

First published by Kingfisher 2005
2 4 6 8 10 9 7 5 3 1

Text copyright © Kingfisher 2005
Illustrations copyright © Jessie Eckel 2005
Created and produced by The Complete Works
St Mary's Road, Royal Leamington Spa, Warwickshire, CV31 1JP UK

A CIP catalogue record for this book is available from the British Library.

ISBN-10: 0 7534 1190 3 ISBN-13: 978 0 7534 1190 2

Printed in China
1TR/0605/SNPEXL/MA(MA)/128MA/F

How to be a Princess

in 7 days or less

Illustrated by Jessie Eckel

Text by Lesley Rees

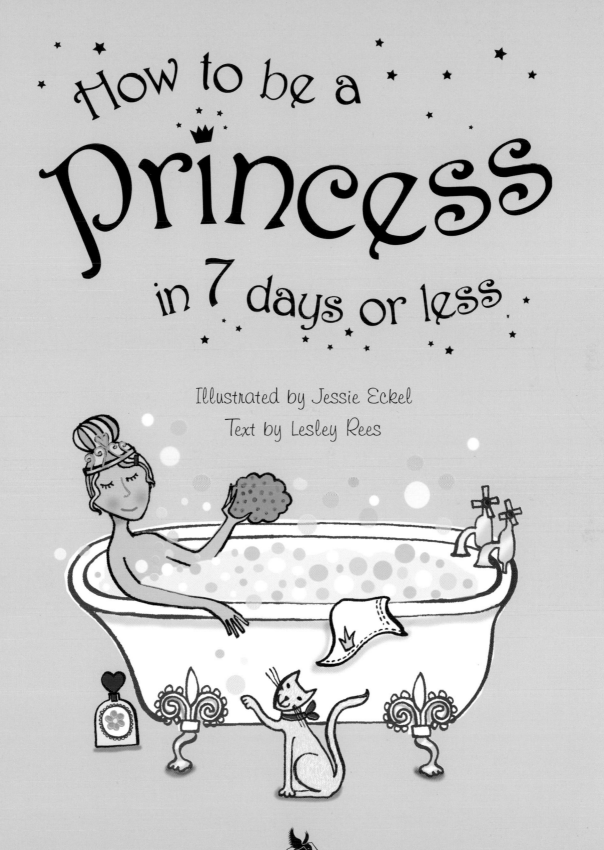

KINGFISHER

Calling All Princesses!

Hi, I'm Princess Emily. Do you want to be a princess like me?
Well, I can show you how! I'm going to give you a complete princess
makeover in just seven days and we'll end up with a fab party to celebrate.
So read on, girls, it's easier than you think!

I live in a palace with my royal family. There's my mum (who's the queen, of course) and my dad (you've guessed it, the king). Dad spends all day watching out for wicked witches and fiery dragons (yeah right, what century is he living in?). My baby sister, Cassie, is a P.I.T. – that's a Princess In Training!

When I grow up, I suppose I'll be queen – how cool is that? But in the meantime, I'm happy being me.

my bedroom

Cassie's bedroom

gardener

chef

maid

Mum

Dad

Cassie

Me

lady-in-waiting

Sparkle

Any girl can be a princess. She doesn't have to reside in a castle or palace – princesses can live anywhere. Remember Rapunzel? She lived in a tiny room at the top of a tall tower, with nothing to do all day but plait her hair.

plait

plait

sweep

sweep

And Snow White lived in a little cottage in the middle of a wood, sweeping, baking and keeping house for the seven dwarfs.

So as you can see, where you live isn't important. But what you *do* need is a really cool bedroom, a fabulous sense of style and, most importantly, the right attitude. Luckily, I'm here to show you how to get them!

Tiara tips

Fashion fun

Beauty make & do

Bedroom D.I.Y.

Get Decorating, Girls!

Day 1

OK, princesses, today is D-Day (that's D for Decorating).
You might not live in a posh palace with a gazillion rooms, but
you can still give your bedroom a royal makeover. Just be sure
to get the king and queen's permission before you begin!

My bedroom is very princessy and pink. But it's not just
one shade of pink – I used lots of different ones.

Prince Charming

Why not put a "throw"
over your bed or chair?

It's so easy to give your room a quick
makeover – just change the colour of your
duvet cover, curtains or cushions.

I have pretty white curtains and lots of purple and silver
cushions on my bed – plus my teddy. Well, a princess needs
someone to confide in and cuddle!

Remember, darker colours make
rooms look smaller.

All princesses need their beauty sleep!

Hanging lace curtains over your bed will make you feel like Sleeping Beauty.

Mirror, mirror on the wall, who has the best bedroom of them all?

A dressing table is a great place to keep your jewellery box and sparkly nail varnish. If you don't have a dressing table, don't worry – a small bedside table or shelf will do just as well.

A princess can never have too many clothes!

If you don't have much space, try putting your clothes and shoes away in a cupboard – your room will look bigger and you'll make the queen happy at the same time!

Above all, a princess's bedroom should show who she is. Even if you share your room, you can create a special space that reflects your personality and highlights your great taste.

Sparkly Surprises

Today we're going to make your fab bedroom look even better. You'll find everything you need to make these fun projects in the Royal Kitchen. They're guaranteed to make your room fit for a princess!

You've Been Framed

First of all take...

- ♥ an empty cereal box
- ♥ scissors
- ♥ glue
- ♥ paint and paintbrush
- ♥ dry macaroni pasta
- ♥ glitter
- ♥ two photos

What you do next...

1. Take the cereal box and carefully cut off the top, sides and bottom.

2. Fold the front in half widthways – the plain side should face the outside with the fold at the top.

Glue here.

3. Open the card up and put glue on the inside.

4. Now fold the card again and firmly press together until stuck.

5. When the glue has dried, fold the card in half lengthways then open it up. It should stand up like an open book.

6. Paint both sides of the card in your favourite colours and leave to dry.

7. Paint pieces of macaroni in pretty colours and sprinkle on glitter while still wet. Leave to dry.

8. Next, take two photos and carefully spread a little glue onto the back of each one. Place a photo on each side of the card and press down gently.

9. Now glue the painted macaroni around the photos to decorate your new frame.

I made a frame for my fave pics of Prince Charming and Sparkle.

The Princess is In

Now let's make a sign to hang over your door handle to tell everyone whether you're in or out. You'll need all the things you used to make your photo frame, plus a cup, a pencil and some pens.

What you do next...

1. Take the cereal box and carefully cut off the top, sides and bottom.

2. Take the front or back piece and fold it in half lengthways. The plain side of the card should face you, and the fold should be on the left.

3. Take a cup and place it on the card, making sure it's centred and about 1cm down from the top.

4. Draw around it so you have a circle shape.

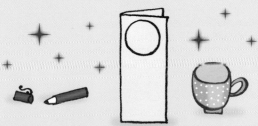

5. Open the card up and put glue on the inside.

6. Fold the card back over again, pressing firmly to stick both sides together.

7. Carefully cut the circle out, making sure you cut through both layers of card. You may need an adult to help you do this.

8. Paint both sides and leave to dry.

9. On one side of the sign write HRH (your name) IS IN!

10. On the other side, write HRH (your name) IS OUT!

11. Then decorate both sides with glitter and stickers and hang over your door handle. You're now ready to receive guests – or go out!

glue glue

HRH means Her Royal Highness.

ring ring

HRH EMILY IS OUT!

A Princess Party

Day 3

Princesses just want to have fun, and what could be more fun than throwing a party? By the end of this week you'll "graduate" from being a P.I.T. to a proper princess. So why not celebrate by hosting a party for all your princess pals?

Perfect Party Invites

Remember how excited Cinderella was when her invitation to the ball arrived? Getting a party invite is a thrill – sending them is, too.

First of all take...

- ♥ an empty cereal box
- ♥ coloured pens
- ♥ scissors
- ♥ paper
- ♥ glitter
- ♥ stickers

What you do next...

1. Take the cereal box and draw a tiara shape onto it. Have a look at the tiara that came with this book for an idea of the shape.

2. Cut the tiara out and use it as a template.

3. Place the template on a sheet of paper and draw around it. Repeat to make several tiara shapes.

4. Cut out the tiara shapes.

5. Now write out the invitations. They could say something like…

> Princess (your name)
> Requests the pleasure of Princess
> (your friend's name)
> At a Princess Party
> On (put the party date here)
> At (put the party time and place here)
> Don't forget to wear your tiara!
> RSVP

6. Finally, decorate with coloured pens, glitter and stickers. Now you can give or post them to all your princess friends.

RSVP is French for "Please reply".

You can invite a few handsome princes if you want. But they can be a bit greedy, so make sure your servants guard the cakes.

Yum yum!

Boys!

Cinderella had great fun at her party, dancing with Prince Charming. But when the clock struck midnight, she had to run!

Don't forget to be home by midnight.

dance

dance

Sleeping Beauty had to wait a long time for her chance to party – a hundred years! Luckily, you only have to wait four more days.

Only 91 years to go!

The Sparkly Stuff

Now girls, it's time for us to check out the sparkly stuff!
Do you have a huge collection of necklaces, rings and earrings?
A princess can never have too many jewels. Of course, you can't
wear them all at once, so here's where you can keep them.

Day 4

Emily's Jewellery Box

First of all take...

- ♥ PVA glue
- ♥ paint
- ♥ paintbrush
- ♥ glitter
- ♥ stickers / jewels

- ♥ an old shoe box or ice cream carton
- ♥ 4 plastic lids from cans of hairspray or furniture polish

What you do next...

1. Pour some PVA glue into a container. Add the paint, drop by drop, and mix with the paintbrush until you get the colour you want.

2. Sprinkle in some glitter.

3. Now paint the glue mixture all over your shoe box or carton, both outside and in, as well as on both sides of the lid. When it's dry, the glue will make the box look shiny and the glitter will make it sparkle.

4. When your shoe box or carton is dry, paint the top of the four plastic lids with plain PVA glue and stick them down in each corner of your box to make little cups. These will be perfect for holding rings and earrings.

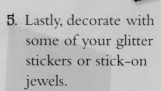

5. Lastly, decorate with some of your glitter stickers or stick-on jewels.

Now you can fill your jewellery box with all your baubles, bracelets and bangles. Why not make one as a gift for the queen or for one of your princess pals?

glitter

glitter

Try not to touch the back of your jewels so they stay sticky.

If your new jewellery box is looking a bit empty, just use the jewel earrings that came with this book for instant sparkle. Simply peel a jewel off the paper and position it on your earlobe. Press it gently to fix it in place. Pick earrings that match your clothes or eye colour.

Princess Tresses

The next step to becoming a princess is good hair care. Rapunzel kept her long locks in tip-top condition, which was handy when her handsome prince needed a ladder to climb up! You can use the hair elastics that came with this book to try out these princessy styles.

Pretty Plait

If your hair is long, an easy way to keep it looking neat is to plait it.

1. Brush all of your hair to the back of your head and gather it up at your neck.

2. Now divide it into three sections – like this, ok?

3. Take the right section and cross it over the middle section. See how the right section has now become the middle?

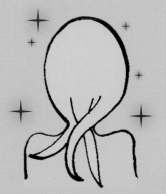

4. Then take the left section and cross it over the middle section.

5. Then cross the right section over the middle section, so it becomes the middle section again.

6. Keep going until all of your hair is in one long plait, then tie it with a hair elastic.

7. Now tie a ribbon around the end of your plait and pull the plait upwards. The plait forms a loop, with the end underneath.

8. Take the ribbon up on either side of the plait and tie in a bow over the top.

It might seem hard at first, but remember: every time you cross a left or right section over the middle section, it becomes the middle. If you keep practising, you'll soon get the hang of it.

Twirl Time

Princess Carly loves to style her shoulder-length tresses with pretty hair clips.

1. First of all, brush your hair. Then take a small section and "twirl" it round and round until it looks like a small rope.

2. Pull the "rope" sideways or backwards tightly, and use a hair clip to fix the end of the "rope" to the rest of your hair.

3. Now take another section of hair next to it and do it all over again. This is a really good way of tying back your fringe or the sides of your hair.

Short 'n' Sweet

Princesses with short hair have so many style options. Here are just a few great party hairdos.

1. Take a little bunch of hair in one hand and a hair elastic in the other hand.

2. Pop the elastic over the hair and push it to the base of the bunch. Twist and pop it over again until it's tight enough to hold your hair in place. Repeat until all your hair is in bunches.

Princess Courtney looks so glamorous with her hair in tiny bunches.

Princess Britney loves using sparkly hair gel to "mould" her hair into spikes.

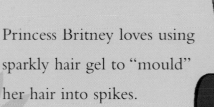

Princess Chelsea likes to slick back her hair with wet-look gel so that it lies sleek and flat to her head. She always pulls down a piece of her fringe and gels it into a kiss-curl.

Looking Good, Girls!

Because they always try to look their best, princesses need lots of clothes. You might not have a fairy godmother to wave a magic wand and help you dress, but you've got me! Let's see what outfits you should wear for different occasions.

A wonderful long dress and a tiara is the perfect outfit to wear to Prince Charming's Ball.

Whoops-a-daisy!

Long dresses require poise and practice — aaagh!

I'm not looking!

It's time for tea with the Queen Mum. A short dress or a pretty skirt and blouse is just right. I always throw a wrap around my shoulders — it smartens up any outfit, even my jeans.

It's a wrap!

Tankini or bikini?

Sarongs are hip.

I love going to the beach and hanging out with my friends. Remember to pack the sunscreen!

SPARKLE CITY

When I've finished soaking up the sun, I like to hit the shops in a pair of shorts and a t-shirt. Any colour will do – but I usually go for pink. Cool shades complete my look!

Use a scarf as a belt – very princessy!

Shop till you drop!

Choices, choices!

Accessories are a great way to give old clothes a new twist. The right bags, belts, hats and shoes can really make an outfit.

So, what should you wear to your party? Whatever makes you feel good – it's your party!

Royal Etiquette

Your tiara and impeccable manners show everyone you're a princess.
Your tiara is not just for formal occasions; you can wear it almost
anywhere – except when you're in bed or washing your hair!
Here's a handy guide to when you should and shouldn't wear your tiara.

Riding class: it doesn't
fit over the helmet!

To a party: any
party, any time!

Doing homework:
it helps me think.

Gym class: standing on
your head is too painful!

Swimming: OK
for pool parties,
not so good for
scuba diving!

To the cinema: it
might be a premiere.

Wearing your tiara should make you feel like a princess, so you'd better behave like one. Getting into a car should be elegant – not a scramble.

1. First, get your chauffeur to open the door.
2. Facing outwards, sink slowly down onto the seat – no collapsing!

3. Then swivel round, bending both legs at the same time with your ankles together, and lift your legs into the car.
4. Sit up straight with your hands on your lap. Now you're good to go!

Princesses also need to know how to wave properly. You should greet your subjects with an elegant and graceful motion – not like you're trying to direct traffic!

See, it's easy.

dab
dab

A princess should have beautiful table manners. She never chews with her mouth open (yuck, how gross would that be?). Unlike some princes, she always uses her napkin and not her sleeve to wipe her mouth. Most importantly, she never forgets to say "please" and "thank you".

Princess Party Food

The invitations have gone out and you know what you're wearing, but what are you going to feed your party guests? A princess doesn't want to spend hours working in the kitchen, so here are some quick and delicious recipes to prepare in advance.

Princess Punch

First of all take...

- ♥ lemonade
- ♥ a large jug
- ♥ strawberry or blackcurrant cordial
- ♥ a knife
- ♥ apples
- ♥ grapes
- ♥ strawberries
- ♥ ice cubes
- ♥ glasses

Sparkle! Fizz! Pop!

What you do next...

1. Pour the lemonade into a jug.

2. Add strawberry or blackcurrant cordial and stir until it's the perfect shade of pink.

3. Carefully chop the apples into chunks.

4. Pop the apple chunks, grapes and strawberries in the jug and add ice cubes.

5. Serve in pretty glasses, making sure everyone gets some fruit.

Tasty and healthy!

— Sparkly Biscuits —

First of all take...

- a spoon
- icing sugar
- a bowl
- water
- red food colouring
- biscuits
- a plate
- sprinkles & silver balls

What you do next...

1. Spoon some icing sugar into a clean bowl and add some water.

2. Mix until smooth. Don't worry if the mixture looks too thin, just add a little more icing sugar and stir. If it's too thick, just add a little more water. The mixture should coat the back of your spoon and drip off easily.

3. Now add red food colouring, a drop at a time, until it's the perfect shade of pink.

4. Drizzle some pink icing over each biscuit.

5. Place the biscuits on a plate and shake on the sprinkles and silver balls.

6. Refrigerate until the icing has set.

Why not put your friends' initials on the biscuits?

— Cheesy Delights —

First of all take...

- a knife
- cheese
- cocktail sticks
- grapes
- an orange
- a plate

What you do next...

1. Cut the cheese into chunks.

2. Take a cocktail stick and, carefully holding it at one end, push a grape onto it.

3. Now take a chunk of cheese and push that onto the stick, too.

4. Take another grape and pop it on the top.

5. Now push the cocktail stick into half an orange and start all over again.

Easy-peasy and cheesy!

Yum Yum

You could use other fruits if you prefer – like pineapple or mango chunks. Just be careful when you're cutting them up, OK?

Party Games

Just one day to go until you can eat all of that yummy food, twirl around in your best party dress and play all kinds of cool games. In case you don't know what party games princesses like to play, here are a few fun ideas.

— Kiss the Frog —

Draw a big frog on a piece of paper and stick it to the wall. Each princess takes turns to put on lip gloss and a blindfold. Then she spins around three times before trying to kiss the frog on his lips. Each princess's name is written next to her "lip-print" and the one who smooches Froggy on his big kissy lips is the winner!

Mmm, strawberry lip gloss – my fave!

Cinderella says… you're out!

— Cinderella Says —

Choose one person to be Cinderella. She's a princess, so she gives everyone commands like "Cinderella says… touch your tiara" or "Cinderella says… curtsy". Everyone must do as Cinderella commands. But if she doesn't say "Cinderella says…" you mustn't do it, or you're out!

— Hunt the Poison Apple —

Hide chocolate coins and a red apple – like the one the Wicked Queen gave to Snow White – around your house. Ask your princess guests to hunt for them. When someone finds a chocolate, they can eat it. The real winner is the one who finds the apple, which can be swapped for a prize.

Gotcha!

Choc-a-licious!

– Ditch the Witch –

Everyone sits in a circle and one princess holds an apple. When the music starts, the princesses pass the apple around until the music stops. Then, whoever is holding the apple isn't a princess – she's a wicked witch! Everyone shouts "Ditch the witch!" and that person is out. Start again and keep going until there's only one princess left.

Ditch the witch!

Z
Z Z

Princess Pamper Time

Day 1

At last the big day has arrived, fellow princesses! It's time to get ready for your party. A princess should always smell as fresh as a daisy, even after a hard day at princess school. A relaxing bubble bath is a great way to pamper yourself.

I love loads of frothy bubbles. In fact, I have my very own bubble bath, which my little sister, Cassie, is not allowed to use! If you would like to make your own, here's how.

Emily

Rub-a-dub-dub, there's a princess in the tub!

Easy-Peasy Bubble Bath

First of all take...

- an empty bottle
- a cup of unscented shampoo
- a cup of water
- 1 teaspoon salt
- essential oil
- 2 drops of red food colouring

What you do next...

1. Find an empty plastic bottle.
2. Pour the shampoo in.
3. Add the water and mix carefully.
4. Add the salt and stir it all up until it goes thick.

5. Now add the essential oil, drop by drop, until it smells as strong as you want – don't put too much in at once, though.

Mix it up and make it nice!

6. Add the red food colouring a drop at a time. Mix until pink.

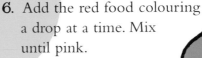

7. Lastly, tie a pretty ribbon around the top and *voila* – your very own princess bubble bath.

You can use your sparkly stickers to decorate the bottle. Now all you have to do is pour some of your bubble bath in while the water is running and you'll have lots of relaxing bubbles.

Now it's time to get dressed for the party!

You've Made It!

Wow, wasn't that just the busiest week ever? But all your hard work was worth it. You've made it to your graduation party and you're now officially a princess. Congratulations! Remember, a princess's work is never done. We have high standards to maintain!

Now that I've taught you how to be a princess it's up to you to keep it going. Being a true princess is about being beautiful on the inside as well as the outside. A princess is nice to her parents, thoughtful to her friends, polite to her teachers and kind to animals.

A true princess stands out from the crowd because, deep down, she knows that wherever she is and whatever she's doing, she's just lucky to be herself.

Princesses rule – OK!

Enough of the serious stuff! What every true princess *also* knows is that a girl can never have too many gorgeous dresses and jewels. As for tiaras, well, what can I tell you? It's part of the uniform! Right, girls?

Anyway, thanks for letting me share my secrets with you. It's been fun. Bye, princesses – keep sparkling!

PRINCESS EMILY'S RULES

1. A princess can never have too many beautiful clothes or shoes.
2. Don't forget to wear your tiara.
3. Princesses are always polite.
4. Always treat the king and queen with respect.
5. Princesses love pressies – but always remember to say "thank you".
6. Princesses should smell as pretty as they look, so hit that shower, girls.
7. Someday your prince will come – believe me.
8. A smile is a princess's most dazzling accessory.
9. We are all princesses inside.
10. Think princess – and you'll be one!

Think princess!